# Paleo Diet Recipes

*Effortless Meals and Grain-Free Recipes to Reboot or Maintain your Health*

## Ariana Barker

work can be in any fashion deemed liable for any hardship or damages that may befall them after undertaking information described herein.

Additionally, the information in the following pages is intended only for informational purposes and should thus be thought of as universal. As befitting its nature, it is presented without assurance regarding its prolonged validity or interim quality. Trademarks that are mentioned are done without written consent and can in no way be considered an endorsement from the trademark holder.

# TABLE OF CONTENTS

# INTRODUCTION

Congratulation on purchasing this book.

The Paleo Diet is a dietary philosophy inspired by the nutritional regimen of humans who lived before agriculture and animal breeding, about 10,000 years ago.

The Paleo Diet does not require any kind of calculation, estimation, or planning. It allows eating whenever the appetite arises, as long as only "paleo" foods are consumed: game, eggs, fish, reptiles, worms, insects, berries, vegetables, fruits (less than vegetables), roots, bulbs, oilseeds, etc. More rarely, shellfish, mollusks, very sweet fruits, and honey.

The paleo-diet rejects the use of dietary supplements, milk and dairy products, cereals, legumes, salt, sugar, fats for seasoning, food additives (or foods containing them), sweet drinks, preserved and processed foods.

The adaptation of the paleo diet to contemporary needs and tastes includes greater use of meat (especially white), fish products, and oil for seasoning.

The benefits come from not having too much sugar or refined and industrial foods. The absence of preservatives, dyes, and chemical additives and the abundance of fresh, lightly seasoned, and unprocessed foods is good for the body, which in the early days will feel a burst of energy.

# PALEO RECIPES

# FREEDOM WAFFLES

Time required:
25 minutes

Servings: 04

## INGREDIENTS

*2 large eggs*

*¼ cup almond or coconut milk*

*1½ cups almond flour*

*1 teaspoon sea salt*

*1 teaspoon baking soda*

*Dash of cinnamon*

## STEPS FOR COOKING

1. Preheat your waffle iron to your desired setting.
2. Whisk the eggs and milk together until foamy. You may find a hand mixer makes this easier.
3. Thoroughly combine all the remaining dry ingredients together in a separate bowl.
4. Add the egg/milk mixture into the bowl with the combined dry ingredients and mix until smooth.
5. Put 1/4 cup of the batter into the preheated waffle iron.
6. Cook until golden brown and then remove.
7. Top with fresh fruit of your choice and/or almond butter.

# BANANA FRITTERS

Time required:
25 minutes

Servings: 04

## INGREDIENTS

*2 plantains*
*1 teaspoon cinnamon*
*1 pinch of salt*
*6 tbsp coconut oil*

## STEPS FOR COOKING

1. First, peel the plantains and grate them. Now mix the rasps with cinnamon.

2. Melt 2 tablespoons of coconut oil in a pan, then shape circles out of the rasps and place them in the pan.

3. After about 2 minutes, turn and add coconut oil again until all of their buffers are baked out.

# Banana and Avocado Nut Smoothie

Time required:
10 minutes

Servings: 01

## INGREDIENTS

*1 cup Almond milk*

*1 Avocado (cubed)*

*1 large Banana
(broken into chunks)*

*3 tablespoons
Peanut butter*

*2 cubes Ice cubes*

*1 teaspoon Vanilla
extract*

*Mint leaves, for
garnish*

## STEPS FOR COOKING

1. Begin by adding almond milk, banana, avocado, peanut butter, vanilla extract, and ice cubes to a blender.

2. Blend into a smooth, puree-like consistency. Make sure all ingredients are well incorporated.

3. Transfer into a tall glass and garnish with mint leaves.

4. Enjoy!

# Avocado Toast

Time required:
10 minutes

_____

Servings: 01

## INGREDIENTS

*4 Bread slices (whole-grain)*

*1 Avocado (cut in cubes)*

*2 tablespoons fresh parsley (chopped)*

*1 ½ teaspoon Olive oil (extra-virgin)*

*½ Lemon (juiced)*

*½ teaspoon Salt*

*½ tsp. Pepper Black (ground)*

*½ tsp. Onion powder*

*½ tsp. Garlic powder*

## STEPS FOR COOKING

1. Begin by toasting all 4 bread slices in a toaster oven or toaster.

2. Place the cubed avocado in a bowl and add the parsley, lemon juice, olive oil, pepper, salt, garlic powder, and onion powder.

3. Use a masher or fork to mash and mix avocado with other ingredients.

4. Divide the avocado mixture into 4 equal parts and place one part of the avocado mixture on each of the toast slices.

5. Serve right away!

# SWEET POTATO LATKES

Time required:
35 minutes

Servings: 06

## INGREDIENTS

*5 cups grated sweet potato*

*2 eggs*

*2 tablespoons onions, minced*

*1 teaspoon cinnamon*

*Salt and pepper to taste*

*Coconut oil for frying*

## STEPS FOR COOKING

1. Mix all the ingredients together in a large mixing bowl.

2. Heat a griddle or frying pan over medium heat and melt a spoonful of coconut oil.

3. Take a small amount of the potato mixture and drop it onto the hot griddle or skillet and form little cakes.

4. Cook for 3-5 minutes on each side, cooking until each side is golden brown and heated all the way through.

5. Top the latkes with favorites like fried eggs and bacon if you wish.

# Sweet Potato Omelet with Spinach

Time required:
35 minutes

Servings: 02

## INGREDIENTS

*1 large sweet potato*
*6 eggs*
*1 small onion*
*1 handful of spinach*
*1 pinch of salt*
*3 tbsp ghee for frying*

## STEPS FOR COOKING

1. First, peel the sweet potatoes, cut them into small pieces, and cook them for about 7 minutes until they are firm to the bite.
2. Meanwhile, peel and chop the onion.
3. Now melt the ghee in a pan and fry the onions until translucent. Then add the spinach and sweet potatoes and fry until the spinach collapses.
4. Whisk the eggs, then add them to the pan.
5. Put the lid on the pan and let the eggs sit for a few minutes.
6. Finally, turn the omelet and fry the other side, adding a little more ghee if necessary.

# Sweet Potato and Carrot Pancakes

Time required:
25 minutes

Servings: 10

## INGREDIENTS

*1 large sweet potato*

*1 small onion*

*2 carrots*

*2 eggs*

*1 pinch of salt*

*1 pinch of pepper*

## STEPS FOR COOKING

1. First, peel the sweet potato, carrots, and onion and grate them in a food processor.
2. Then mix in the eggs and refine it with salt and pepper. Then heat your pan and add the potato and carrot sauce.

# CHOCOLATE GRANOLA CRUNCH

Time required:
35 minutes

Servings: 08

## INGREDIENTS

½ cup raw sunflower seeds

½ cup raw pumpkin seeds

1 cup almond meal

1 cup unsweetened shredded coconut

2 cups raw almonds, slivered or chopped

2 tablespoons unsweetened cacao powder

Pinch of ground cinnamon

½ cup coconut oil

½ cup raw honey

1 teaspoon pure vanilla extract

## STEPS FOR COOKING

1. Preheat your oven to 325 degrees F.
2. Line a cookie sheet with a piece of aluminum foil that is lightly greased.
3. Take a large mixing bowl and combine the sunflower seeds, pumpkin seeds, almond meal, coconut, almonds, cacao powder, and cinnamon.
4. In a microwave-safe bowl, combine the remaining ingredients of oil, honey, and vanilla.
5. Place the bowl of wet ingredients into the microwave and microwave on high for 20 to 30 seconds to warm it up. This will allow your mixture to pour easily.
6. Place the wet ingredients into the dry ingredients and stir well. Be sure everything is evenly coated.

| INGREDIENTS | STEPS FOR COOKING |
|---|---|
| | 7. Place the mixture onto your foil-lined cookie. |
| | 8. Spread evenly over the cookie sheet. |
| | 9. Place the cookie sheet into the oven and bake for 25 minutes, being careful that the mixture doesn't burn. (You may want to stir it once during the process so it cooks evenly). |
| | 10. Now remove the cookie sheet from the oven and allow the crunch to cool. You will find this mixture gets crunchy as it gets colder. |
| | 11. This recipe can be used in place of a grain cereal by putting it into a bowl with some nut milk or eaten plain. |

# Breakfast Sausage

Time required:
25 minutes

Servings: 04

## INGREDIENTS

2 pounds ground beef

1 pound ground pork

2 teaspoons fresh thyme, chopped

2 teaspoons fresh sage, chopped

1 teaspoon fresh rosemary, chopped

2 teaspoons sea salt

1½ teaspoons black pepper

1 teaspoon fresh grated nutmeg

½ teaspoon cayenne

## STEPS FOR COOKING

1. Begin by combining all of your ingredients in a large mixing bowl.

2. Form the meat mixture into little round balls or links, 1 to 2 inches in diameter.

3. Heat a frying pan or skillet on your stovetop over a medium setting using a small amount of coconut oil in the bottom.

4. Carefully place the meat rounds in the pan and cook for 10 to 15 minutes until they are browned and cooked through.

5. Remove the meat from the pan and drain any excess oil or grease. A perfect companion for your pancakes, waffles, or eggs.

# Egg Crepes with Avocados

Time required:
35 minutes

Servings: 04

## STEPS FOR COOKING

1. Heat olive oil over medium heat in a pan and crack in the eggs.
2. Spread the eggs lightly with the spatula and cook for about 3 minutes on both sides.
3. Dish out the egg crepe and top with turkey breast, alfalfa sprouts, and avocado.
4. Roll up tightly and serve warm.

# COCONUT CREPES

Time required:
18 minutes

Servings: 03

## INGREDIENTS

15 grams Virgin Coconut Oil

¼ cup, Almond Milk

¼ cup, Coconut Milk

¼ grams, Vanilla Essence

30 grams, Coconut Flour

15 grams, Almond Meal

1 cup Applesauce

## STEPS FOR COOKING

1.  Dump all of your ingredients into one large bowl and whisk until smooth. Then set aside for ten minutes to allow the liquid to absorb into the flour. In the meantime, lightly oil a frying pan on the stove, and pour in the batter, and spread until the pan is coated with a thin layer.

2.  Cook until the crepe starts to get crispy, and flip. Another minute on the stove, and you are ready to serve alongside your toppings of choice or course.

# RHUBARB ASPARAGUS

Time required:
20 minutes

Servings: 04

## INGREDIENTS

500g white asparagus
300g rhubarb
2 tbsp olive oil
2 tbsp lemon juice
1 tbsp honey
1 pinch of salt and pepper

## STEPS FOR COOKING

1. First, peel the asparagus and remove the ends. Then cook the asparagus for about 10 minutes.

2. Meanwhile, you can peel the rhubarb and cut it into small pieces.

3. Now put some olive oil in a pan and sauté the rhubarb for about 5 minutes. Then add lemon juice, honey, salt, and pepper and let it simmer briefly.

4. Then serve the asparagus with the rhubarb.

# PALEOLITHIC MAYONNAISE

Time required:
15 minutes

Servings: 04

## INGREDIENTS

2 tablespoons freshly squeezed lemon juice

2 large eggs

1 teaspoon dry mustard

Salt to taste. Start with 1 teaspoon

1/4 teaspoon cayenne pepper (optional)

2 cups olive oil

## STEPS FOR COOKING

1. In a blender, place the lemon juice, eggs, dry mustard, salt, and cayenne (if using).

2. Pulse for a few seconds until the mixture becomes frothy.

3. Turn your blender on a low setting and allow it to keep running.

4. Slowly add the oil—almost a drop at a time—to the mixture until it begins to emulsify.

5. Keep adding the oil slowly until it is all blended in.

6. Add salt to taste.

7. Store in a container in your refrigerator.

# CREAM OF BROCCOLI SOUP

Time required:
25 minutes

Servings: 04

## INGREDIENTS

*1 tsp EVOO*

*1 yellow onion, sliced thin*

*1 head cauliflower*

*3 cups plain almond milk*

*3 cups broccoli, finely chopped*

*1 tbsp. onion powder*

## STEPS FOR COOKING

1. Cook the onions in the oil in a large saucepan, then season and cook until golden and soft. Add the cauliflower and almond milk, then cover and boil.

2. Drop the heat to a simmer and cook the mixture until the florets are soft, 8-10 minutes. Add half of the broccoli and warm through.

3. Pour the mixture for the soup into a blender, then puree until very smooth. Return the puree to the pot.

4. Add the onion powder and the rest of the broccoli. Season and cook, covered, on low heat for 10-12 minutes, until the soup is thick and creamy.

5. Serve warm.

# MIXED CABBAGE COLESLAW

Time required:
10 minutes

Servings: 04

## INGREDIENTS

1 cup paleo
mayonnaise

¼ tsp ground black
pepper

4 oz. kale

½ tsp salt

8 oz. green cabbage

4 oz. red cabbage

## STEPS FOR COOKING

1. Using a mandolin slicer, sharp knife, or a food processor, slice the cabbage into pieces.

2. Move into a bowl and then add the pepper, mayonnaise, and salt.

3. Properly stir it and give it 10 (ten) minutes for it to settle.

# Chicken Lime Soup

Time required:
55 minutes

Servings: 08

## INGREDIENTS

*6 chicken thighs, skinless and boneless*

*2 tablespoons olive oil*

*1 medium-sized white onion, peeled and chopped*

*6 teaspoons minced garlic*

*2 chipotle chiles, chopped*

*2 tablespoons adobo sauce*

*48 fluid ounce chicken broth*

*½ cup chopped cilantro*

## STEPS FOR COOKING

1. Rinse chicken pieces, pat dry and cut into 1-inch pieces, set aside until required.

2. Place a large pot over medium-low heat, add oil and let heat. Add onion and garlic and cook for 5-7 minutes or until onion is nicely golden brown.

3. Switch heat to high, push onion and garlic to the side of the pan and then add chicken to the pot. Cook for 5 minutes or until chicken is nicely golden brown, stir occasionally.

4. Add chipotle peppers, adobo sauce, and chicken broth and stir until just mixed. Switch heat to low and simmer the soup for 15 minutes, skim off any foam.

## INGREDIENTS

*2 limes, juiced*

*1 ½ teaspoon salt*

*½ teaspoon ground black pepper*

*1 medium-sized avocado, peeled and pitted*

*Crushed tortilla chips for serving*

## STEPS FOR COOKING

5. After 15 minutes of cooking, adjust the seasoning and stir in cilantro and lime juice.

6. Ladle soup into serving bowls, top with avocado slices and tortilla chips, and serve.

# ALMOND AND CARROT SALAD

Time required:
10 minutes

Servings: 04

## INGREDIENTS

6 carrots

1 green apple

2 tbsp lemon juice

6 tbsp coconut milk

50g almonds

1 pinch of salt and pepper

## STEPS FOR COOKING

1.  First peel the carrots, core, and cut the apple, and grate them roughly together with the almonds, preferably in a food processor.

2.  Mix the mixture with lemon juice and coconut milk and season with salt and pepper.

# DANDELION AND WALNUT SALAD

Time required:
25 minutes

Servings: 04

## INGREDIENTS

1 handful of
dandelion leaves

1 handful of wild
herbs

2 hands full of leaf
salads

80g walnuts

For the dressing:

2 tbsp olive oil

Juice of one lemon

50g berries

1 tbsp honey

1 pinch of salt and
pepper

## STEPS FOR COOKING

1. First, wash the dandelion leaves, herbs, and lettuce and spin dry. Then roast the walnuts in a pan without oil.

2. Simply mix all the ingredients for the dressing together, then mix the salad with the dressing and pour the walnuts on top.

# Fruity Salad with Chicken

Time required:
15 minutes

Servings: 04

## INGREDIENTS

*12 ounces of canned white chicken*

*2 celery stalks, finely chopped*

*¼ cup chopped red onion*

*¼ cup Paleolithic mayonnaise*

*½ cup dried unsweetened cranberries*

*¼ cup chopped pecans (optional)*

## STEPS FOR COOKING

1. In a medium-sized bowl, put the chicken, celery, onion, mayo cranberries and pecans (if desired).
2. Mix thoroughly.
3. Enjoy plain or make a wrap using lettuce leaves. I also like to use it as a dip with carrot chips, apple slices and even celery sticks.

# POACHED EGG SALAD

Time required:
23 minutes

Servings: 04

## INGREDIENTS

*4 eggs*

*3 tablespoons lemon juice*

*2 teaspoons Dijon mustard*

*¾ teaspoon sea salt*

*½ teaspoon fresh ground pepper*

*½ cup olive oil*

*4 ounces lean ground beef*

*6 cups mixed greens*

*4 ounces aged shredded cheddar cheese, (optional)*

## STEPS FOR COOKING

1. Poach eggs in an egg poacher, saucepan or microwave.

2. Cook until the egg whites are set but the yolks are still runny—about 4 minutes in an egg poacher or 2 minutes in the microwave.

3. To make the dressing, combine the lemon juice, mustard, salt and pepper in a blender.

4. Pour into a medium bowl and slowly whisk in the olive oil until the dressing thickens.

5. Set aside.

6. Place a frying pan over medium heat, saute the beef until browned.

7. Toss the mixed greens with the dressing.

8. Sprinkle with the ground beef and shredded cheese.

| INGREDIENTS | STEPS FOR COOKING |
|---|---|
| | 9. Finally, place one egg on top of each serving of salad. |

# DELICIOUS GARLIC TOMATOES

Time required:
60 minutes

Servings: 04

## INGREDIENTS

4 garlic cloves,
crushed

1 pound mixed
cherry tomatoes

3 thyme sprigs,
chopped

Pinch of sunflower
seeds

Black pepper as
needed

¼ cup olive oil

## STEPS FOR COOKING

1. Preheat your oven to 325°F.
2. Take a baking dish and add tomatoes, olive oil, and thyme.
3. Season with sunflower seeds and pepper and mix.
4. Bake for 50 minutes.
5. Divide tomatoes and pan juices and serve.

# CASHEW SAUCE

Time required:
5 minutes

Servings: 04

## INGREDIENTS

3 ounces cashew
nuts

¼ cup water

½ cup olive oil

1 tablespoon lemon
juice

½ teaspoon onion
powder

½ teaspoon
sunflower seeds

1 pinch cayenne
pepper

## STEPS FOR COOKING

1. Add nuts to your blender and process.
2. Add other ingredients (except oil) and process until smooth.
3. Add a little bit of oil and puree.
4. Serve as needed!

# OVEN SALMON WITH ASPARAGUS IN A PACKET

Time required: 25 minutes

Servings: 04

## INGREDIENTS

*2 wild salmon fillets*

*Stalks of green asparagus*

*1 handful of cherry tomatoes*

*Juice of half a lemon*

*1 pinch of salt and pepper*

*½ teaspoon thyme*

## STEPS FOR COOKING

1. First, preheat your oven to 180 degrees circulating air.

2. Then fold two boats made of parchment paper so that no juice can escape. Then wash the vegetables and cut them into bite-sized pieces.

3. Now distribute a salmon fillet and half of the vegetables in the packet, drizzle with lemon juice, and season with salt, pepper, and thyme.

4. Now put the packet slightly open in the oven and bake it for about 20 minutes until the salmon is cooked through.

# ROSEMARY POTATOES WITH TURKEY

Time required:
70 minutes

Servings: 02

## INGREDIENTS

**For the Potatoes:**
5 large potatoes
2 rosemary stalks
2 tbsp olive oil
½ teaspoon salt
1 pinch of pepper
**For the Turkey:**
2 turkey legs
½ teaspoon salt
2 tbsp ghee
1 pinch of pepper
1 teaspoon paprika powder
1 teaspoon garlic powder
1 teaspoon of crushed marjoram

## STEPS FOR COOKING

1. First, preheat your oven to 200 degrees.

2. Wash, peel and cut the potatoes into large wedges and place them in a baking dish. Chop the rosemary and put it in the baking dish as well. Then mix this with olive oil, salt, and pepper.

3. Then make a spice paste for the turkey from the spices and the melted ghee. Now put the turkey in the baking dish and coat it with the spice paste.

4. Then put the baking dish in the oven for about 40 minutes.

# Easy Vegetable Soup

Time required:
60 minutes

Servings: 04

## INGREDIENTS

*2 tablespoons coconut oil*

*¼ cup diced onion*

*1 cup thinly sliced carrots*

*1 cup thinly sliced zucchini*

*2 teaspoons fresh parsley*

*¼ teaspoon thyme*

*⅛ teaspoon pepper*

*2 cups water*

## STEPS FOR COOKING

1. In a medium saucepan, heat up the coconut oil.

2. Once heated, add the onion and cook until it is translucent.

3. Add the carrots, zucchini, parsley, thyme and pepper to the saucepan.

4. Cover and cook over low heat until the vegetables are tender— approximately 10 minutes.

5. Add the water and bring to a boil.

6. Reduce the heat to medium and cook until vegetables are soft— approximately 20 minutes.

7. Once you've finished cooking the vegetables, remove the pot from the heat and allow it to cool slightly.

8. Remove ½ cup of soup from the pan and put it aside.

| INGREDIENTS | STEPS FOR COOKING |
|---|---|

9. Pour the remaining soup into a blender and process at a low speed until you've reached a smooth consistency.

10. Combine the pureed mixture and the reserved soup into a saucepan and cook, stirring constantly until it is hot.

11. Serve and enjoy.

# Lobster Bisque Paleo Style

Time required:
25 minutes

Servings: 04

## INGREDIENTS

4 tablespoons ghee

2 tablespoons
scallions, diced

1 stalk celery,
chopped

4 tablespoons
coconut flour

2 cups PLUS 2
tablespoons coconut
milk

1 tablespoon
tomato paste

2 teaspoons paprika

1 teaspoon Old Bay
Seasoning

⅛ teaspoon cayenne
pepper

## STEPS FOR COOKING

1. Melt ghee in a saucepan over medium low heat.

2. Add the scallions and celery and cook for about 3 minutes until the vegetables begin to soften.

3. Add the coconut flour and blend into the vegetables.

4. Cook over medium heat for about 3 minutes, stirring fre q uently.

5. Slowly pour the coconut milk into the vegetable mixture and stir until blended.

6. Now stir in the tomato paste.

7. Cook over medium-low heat for about 5 minutes or until the bisque begins to thicken.

8. Add the paprika, Old Bay Seasoning, cayenne, and broth.

## INGREDIENTS

*2-3 tablespoons chicken broth*

*10 ounces cooked, coarsely chopped lobster meat, drained well*

*Salt and pepper to taste*

## STEPS FOR COOKING

9. Stir to blend.
10. Add the cooked lobster meat.
11. Salt and pepper to taste.
12. Simmer the bisque over low heat for about 5 more minutes until heated through.

# STEAK AND SALSA WRAP

Time required:
15 minutes

Servings: 02

## INGREDIENTS

*1 serving of cooked skirt steak*

*1 tomato, chopped*

*1 avocado, peeled, pitted and cubed*

*1 teaspoon sea salt*

*Juice from ½ lime*

*1 tablespoon apple cider vinegar*

*1 tablespoon olive oil*

*Romaine or leafy lettuce for wraps*

*Favorite salsa*

## STEPS FOR COOKING

1. Place your lettuce leaf on a plate and place the skirt steak on top.

2. Put the tomato and avocado into a bowl.

3. In a small separate bowl, combine the salt, lime juice, vinegar, and oil until mixed well.

4. Pour the liquid mixture over the tomato and avocado and mix gently.

5. Top the steak with the mixture and add your favorite salsa.

# Japanese Cabbage Dish

Time required:
25 minutes

Servings: 06

## INGREDIENTS

*3 tablespoons sesame oil*

*3 tablespoons rice vinegar*

*1 garlic clove, minced*

*1 teaspoon fresh ginger root, grated*

*1 teaspoon sunflower seeds*

*1 teaspoon pepper*

*½ large head cabbage, cored and shredded*

*1 bunch green onions, thinly sliced*

*1 cup almond slivers*

*¼ cup toasted sesame seeds*

## STEPS FOR COOKING

1. Add all listed ingredients to a large bowl, making sure to add the wet ingredients first, followed by the dried ingredients.

2. Toss well to ensure that the cabbages are coated well.

3. Serve and enjoy!

# Baked Chicken Fajitas

Time required:
28 minutes

Servings: 06

## INGREDIENTS

*1 1/2 lbs chicken
tenders*

*2 tbsp fajita
seasoning*

*2 tbsp olive oil*

*1 onion, sliced*

*2 bell pepper, sliced*

*1 lime juice*

*1 tsp kosher salt*

## STEPS FOR COOKING

1. Preheat the oven to 400 F.
2. Add all ingredients to a large mixing bowl, then toss well.
3. Transfer bowl mixture on a baking tray and bake in preheated oven for 15-18 minutes.
4. Serve and enjoy.

# MEXICAN BEEF WITH ZUCCHINI

Time required:
35 minutes

Servings: 06

## INGREDIENTS

1 ½ lbs ground beef

¼ tsp red pepper flakes

½ tsp onion powder

½ tsp ground cumin

½ tbsp chili powder

10 oz salsa

2 garlic cloves, minced

2 zucchinis, diced

½ tsp pepper

1 tsp salt

## STEPS FOR COOKING

1. Brown meat in a pan with garlic, pepper, and salt.
2. Add tomatoes and spices and stir well.
3. Cover and simmer over low heat for 10 minutes, then add remaining ingredients cooking for 10 minutes more.
4. Serve and enjoy.

# Asian Beef Stew

Time required:
5 hours 25 minutes

Servings: 08

## INGREDIENTS

3 lbs beef stew meat, trimmed

2 tsp ginger, minced

2 garlic cloves, minced

1/3 cup tomato paste

14.5 oz can coconut milk

1 medium onion, sliced

2 tbsp olive oil

2 cups carrots, julienned

2 cups broccoli florets

2 tsp fresh lime juice

2 tbsp soy sauce

1/2 cup curry paste

2 Tsp sea salt

## STEPS FOR COOKING

1. Heat 1 tbsp oil in a pan over medium-high heat, then add meat and brown the meat on all sides.

2. Transfer meat to crockpot.

3. Add remaining oil in a pan and sauté ginger, garlic, and onion over medium-high heat for 5 minutes.

4. Add coconut milk and stir well.

5. Transfer pan mixture to the crockpot.

6. Add remaining ingredients except for carrots and broccoli into the crockpot.

7. Cover and cook on high for 5 hours, then add carrots and broccoli during the last 30 minutes of cooking.

8. Serve and enjoy.

# SCALLOPS AND SAUTEED VEGGIES

Time required:
30 minutes

Servings: 04

## INGREDIENTS

½ red onion, thinly sliced

6 slices of thick nitrite/nitrate-free bacon (optional)

3 garlic cloves, minced

1 pound fresh snap peas

3 tablespoons flat leaf parsley, finely diced

Juice from ½ a lemon

½ teaspoon dried thyme

Salt and pepper to taste

2 tablespoons coconut oil

## STEPS FOR COOKING

1. In a frying pan, saute the onions and bacon for 4 minutes.

2. Add the garlic and snap peas and saute for another 2 minutes.

3. Add the parsley, lemon juice, thyme, salt and pepper and cook for another minute.

4. Remove the veggie mixture from the pan and set aside.

5. Add the coconut oil to the skillet and heat over medium-high heat.

6. Make sure your scallops are entirely defrosted and patted dry with paper towels.

7. Sprinkle the scallops with a bit of salt and pepper and sear the scallops for 1 minute on each side (they should be nice and brown).

## INGREDIENTS

*1 pound sea scallops, defrosted*

*½ cup chicken broth*

## STEPS FOR COOKING

8. Add the veggie mixture on top of the scallops, pour the chicken broth over the scallops and gently stir.

9. Bring to a boil and simmer for another minute or two. The scallops should be tender and cooked all the way through. Do not overcook scallops or their texture will become rubbery.

# BALTIMORE CRAB CAKES

Time required:
15 minutes

Servings: 6

## INGREDIENTS

*1 pound crab meat*

*2 tablespoons coconut flour (or enough to make the mixture stick together)*

*1 egg*

*¼ cup minced fresh parsley*

*1 teaspoon crushed garlic*

*¼ cup Paleolithic mayo*

*2 tablespoons spicy mustard*

*Salt and pepper to taste*

## STEPS FOR COOKING

1. If using the canned crab, make sure to crumble the crab with your hands into a large mixing bowl and pick out any shells you might find.

2. Mix the crab with the coconut flour, egg, parsley, garlic, mayo, mustard, salt, pepper, and chipotle powder.

3. In a large skillet, heat the coconut oil over medium heat for about 1 minute.

4. Form the crab cake mixture into palm-sized patties and fry for 2-3 minutes on each side or until they are golden brown.

| INGREDIENTS | STEPS FOR COOKING |
| --- | --- |
| *⅛ teaspoon of chipotle powder*<br>*3-4 tablespoons coconut oil* | |

# Beef Fillet with Vinaigrette

Time required:
25 minutes

Servings: 02

## INGREDIENTS

*2 beef fillets*

*250g mushrooms*

*1 red onion*

*200g bacon cubes*

*1 bunch of chives*

*50ml red wine vinegar*

*100ml olive oil*

*3 cloves of garlic*

*2 teaspoons of Dijon mustard*

*salt and pepper*

*Rapeseed oil for frying*

## STEPS FOR COOKING

1.  First clean and quarter the mushrooms, cut the onions into cubes, and chop the chives. Peel the garlic, press it down with the knife, and stir it together with the vinegar, oil, mustard, salt, and pepper.

2.  Now preheat the oven to 160 degrees.

3.  Now add a little oil to the pan and roast the fillet on all sides with high heat. Insert the thermometer and place it in the oven on a rack until the desired degree of cooking is achieved.

4.  Meanwhile, toast the mushrooms, bacon, and onions over high heat for 4 minutes, turn off the stove and mix in the vinaigrette and chives.

# PORK RAGOUT WITH TOMATOES

Time required:
55 minutes

Servings: 04

## INGREDIENTS

*1 kg of pork goulash*
*1 large onion*
*2 - 3 cloves of garlic*
*3 tbsp olive oil*
*salt and pepper*
*1 tbsp tomato paste*
*200 ml of dry white wine*
*400 ml beef stock*
*2 organic lemons*
*1 tbsp brown sugar*
*400 g of cocktail tomatoes*

## STEPS FOR COOKING

1.  First, peel the onion and garlic and finely dice them.

2.  Now heat 3 tablespoons of oil in a casserole and sear the meat vigorously on all sides.

3.  Add the onions and the garlic, then sauté for 5 mins. Stir in tomato paste and sauté briefly. Then add the wine, stock, and 400ml water. Cover and let simmer for about an hour over medium heat.

4.  Then, add lemon juice, zest, and pieces to the ragout and let it simmer for another 30 minutes.

5.  Finally, add the tomatoes and let them simmer for 2-3 minutes.

# Pork Fillet with Apple and Ginger Sauce

Time required:
35 minutes

Servings: 04

## INGREDIENTS

20g ginger

600g apples

85g sugar

1 tbsp red wine
vinegar

½ dried chili pepper

salt and pepper

8 pork medallions
(approx. 320g)

1 tbsp olive oil

1 stalk of rosemary

## STEPS FOR COOKING

1.  First, peel the ginger and chop it up. Peel and quarter the apples, remove the core, and cut the apple quarters into approx. 1 x 1 cm cubes.

2.  Melt the sugar in a pan over medium heat to light brown caramel and stir in the ginger. Rub it off immediately with the vinegar.

3.  Then add the diced apple and the whole chili pepper. Boil them briefly and cover and simmer over low heat for about 10-15 minutes so that the apples disintegrate easily.

4.  Season to taste with a little sugar, salt, and pepper.

5.  Finely chop the rosemary and then put two pork medallions on a wooden skewer.

| INGREDIENTS | STEPS FOR COOKING |
|---|---|

6. Place the fillet skewers between two layers of cling film and knock them flat with the bottom of a heavy saucepan or pan.

7. Peel off the foil and brush the meat with a little olive oil.

8. Grill them on the hot charcoal grill for about 6-8 minutes on both sides.

9. Season it, sprinkle with the chopped rosemary and serve with the apple-ginger sauce.

# ALMOND CINNAMON BEEF MEATBALLS

Time required:
35 minutes

Servings: 08

## INGREDIENTS

*2 lbs ground beef*

*3 eggs*

*½ cup fresh parsley, minced*

*1 tsp cinnamon*

*1 ½ tsp dried oregano*

*2 tsp cumin*

*1 tsp garlic, minced*

*1 cup almond flour*

*1 medium onion, grated*

*1 tsp pepper*

*2 tsp salt*

## STEPS FOR COOKING

1. Preheat the oven to 400 F.
2. Add all ingredients into the mixing bowl, then mix until well combined.
3. Make small meatballs from the mixture and place them on a greased baking tray and bake for 20-25 minutes.
4. Serve and enjoy.

# HOMEMADE WORCESTERSHIRE SAUCE

Time required:
15 minutes

Servings: 04

## INGREDIENTS

*1 cup apple cider vinegar*

*¼ cup coconut aminos*

*¼ cup Thai fish sauce (optional, but makes it taste great)*

*¼ cup water*

*¼ teaspoon coarse black pepper*

*½ teaspoon dry mustard*

*½ teaspoon onion powder*

*¼ teaspoon ground cinnamon*

*½ teaspoon ground ginger*

*½ teaspoon garlic powder*

## STEPS FOR COOKING

1. Place all the ingredients into a saucepan on your stovetop.
2. Bring to a boil and allow it to simmer for 1 to 2 minutes.
3. Cool and store in a container in your refrigerator.

# TURKEY MEAT TACOS

Time required:
25 minutes

Servings: 06

## INGREDIENTS

2 tablespoons chili powder

1½ teaspoons cumin

1½ tablespoons paprika

1 tablespoon onion powder

2 teaspoons garlic powder

2 teaspoons dried oregano

1 teaspoon red pepper flakes

¼ cup of coconut oil

3 pounds ground turkey

½ cup water

Romaine lettuce leaves

## STEPS FOR COOKING

1. In a small bowl, combine the chili powder, cumin, paprika, onion powder, garlic powder, oregano, and red pepper flakes.
2. In a large skillet, heat the coconut oil.
3. Add the ground turkey and cook until browned.
4. Do not drain li q uid!
5. Now shake about 1/3 of the spice mixture into the turkey and stir thoroughly.
6. Repeat the above step two more times until all the spices are incorporated into the turkey.
7. Add 1/2 cup of water into the turkey and spices.
8. Bring to a boil.

| INGREDIENTS | STEPS FOR COOKING |
|---|---|

*Your favorite salsa*
*Avocado slices*

9. Now reduce the heat, and let it cook for about 15 minutes. This will reduce the amount of li q uid.

10. Remove from the stovetop and allow it to sit for 8 to 10 minutes.

11. While the turkey is resting, line your plate with a lettuce leaf.

12. Now place some of the turkey mixture onto the lettuce leaf, followed by some salsa and avocado slices (if desired).

# MEATY DINNER MUFFINS

Time required:
30 minutes

Servings: 06

## INGREDIENTS

1 (14.5 ounce) can Italian tomatoes, drained

1 onion, peeled

½ teaspoon sage

½ teaspoon thyme

1/8 teaspoon ground nutmeg

¼ teaspoon onion powder

½ teaspoon ground pepper

½ pound ground turkey

2 pounds ground beef

1 egg

## STEPS FOR COOKING

1. Preheat your oven to 375 degrees F.
2. Lightly grease muffin pans with coconut oil.
3. Place drained tomatoes in a food processor along with the onion.
4. In a small bowl, combine the sage, thyme, nutmeg, onion powder, and pepper together and mix thoroughly.
5. In a large separate bowl, mix this seasoning mix into the ground turkey thoroughly to create "sausage."
6. Now add the beef, egg, garlic, seasonings, salt and pepper and the tomato/ onion puree in with the ground turkey.
7. Fill up the muffin tins about three-fourths of the way full with the meat mixture.

## INGREDIENTS

*1 teaspoon garlic powder*

*1 tablespoon Italian seasonings*

*Salt and pepper to taste*

## STEPS FOR COOKING

8. Place in the preheated oven for 30 - 45 minutes.

9. Check for doneness.

# Coconut Mango Yogurt

Time required:
10 minutes

Servings: 02

## INGREDIENTS

200ml coconut milk
200ml almond milk
1 pinch of vanilla
1 tbsp gelatin
1 mango

## STEPS FOR COOKING

1. Peel and core the mango and cut into large pieces. Now puree the mango together with coconut milk and almond milk.

2. Dissolve the gelatine in a little almond milk and heat gently until the gelatine is completely free of lumps.

3. Then puree the gelatine together with the mango to a uniform mass.

4. Pour the yogurt into a glass and put it in the refrigerator for at least an hour.

# CHESTNUT DONUTS

Time required:
20 minutes

Servings: 12

## INGREDIENTS

*40g chestnuts*

*40g ground almonds*

*30g ghee*

*2 tbsp honey*

*1 pinch of ground cloves*

*1 pinch of cinnamon*

## STEPS FOR COOKING

1. Process the chestnuts in the food processor with the spices to a fine flour and add the remaining ingredients.

2. Then let the dough stand in the refrigerator for 1 hour.

3. Preheat the oven to 160 degrees.

4. Roll small balls into sausages, shape them into circles and place them on a baking sheet.

5. Put them in the oven for 10 minutes. Let cool down briefly and serve immediately.

# CARROT CAKE

Time required:
80 minutes

Servings: 06

## INGREDIENTS

### For the Cake:

1 cup almond butter

4 tablespoons pure vanilla extract

6 eggs

2 teaspoons fresh orange juice

8 tablespoons raw honey

4-5 cups shredded carrot

3 cups unsweetened raisins

6 cups almond flour

2 teaspoons nutmeg

2 tablespoons cinnamon

2 teaspoons salt

## STEPS FOR COOKING

1. Preheat your oven to 325 degrees F.

2. In a large bowl, put the almond butter and vanilla and stir until smooth.

3. Add the eggs and combine completely.

4. Now add the orange juice, honey, carrots and raisins and blend.

5. In a separate bowl, mix together the flour, nutmeg, cinnamon, salt, soda, and powder.

6. Now gently combine the wet ingredients with the dry ones.

7. Take 2 (9-inch) cake tins and lightly grease with coconut or olive oil.

8. Divide the batter evenly between the two pans.

9. Place into your preheated oven and bake for 45-50 minutes. (Insert a

2 teaspoons baking soda

2 teaspoons baking powder

*For the Icing:*

1 cup coconut milk

½ cup raw honey

Dash of sea salt

2 tablespoons arrowroot powder

2 tablespoons water

1¼ cups coconut oil

toothpick or cake tester into the middle of each cake to make sure no liquid is present-only crumbs).

10. Allow the cake to cool on a rack for approximately 20 minutes before removing the cakes from the pans.

11. In a medium saucepan, add the coconut milk, honey and salt and stir over medium heat.

12. After blending, reduce the heat, simmer and stir constantly for 10 minutes.

13. Remove from the heat.

14. In a separate bowl, combine arrowroot powder with the water and stir to make a paste.

15. Now stir the arrowroot paste into the coconut milk mixture and heat over medium heat until the mixture thickens.

16. Remove from the heat and place into a bowl that contains the melted coconut oil.

17. Blend thoroughly.

18. Place the mixture into a covered freezer container for 45 minutes.

19. Now remove the container from the freezer and stir. Mixture will be thick.

20. Frost your cake with the coconut icing.

21. Garnish with shredded carrots, coconut flakes and chopped nuts if desired.

# FRUITY SALSA

Time required:
15 minutes

Servings: 02

## INGREDIENTS

*1 mango-peeled, seeded and cubed*

*1 avocado-peeled, pitted, and diced*

*4 medium tomatoes, diced*

*1 jalapeno pepper, seeded and minced*

*½ cup chopped fresh cilantro*

*3 cloves garlic, minced*

*1 teaspoon sea salt*

*2 tablespoons lime juice*

*¼ cup chopped onion*

*3 tablespoons olive or coconut oil*

## STEPS FOR COOKING

1. In a medium bowl, combine the mango cubes, avocado, tomato dices, jalapeno, cilantro, and garlic.

2. Once combined, add the salt, lime juice, onion, and oil.

3. After mixing together, place into your refrigerator for approximately 30 minutes before serving.

# Lemon Bars

Time required:
55 minutes

Servings: 08

## INGREDIENTS

1 cup allulose

3 large eggs

¼ tsp. salt

1 ¾ cups almond flour

3 medium lemons

½ cup almond butter, melted

## STEPS FOR COOKING

1. Set your stove to the temperature of 350° Fahrenheit. Cover an 8-inch cake pan with baking paper and set it to the side.

2. In a big dish, blend 1 cup of the almond flour and the almond butter until fully incorporated. Add the allulose (1/4 cup) and salt (1/8 teaspoon) and combine completely.

3. Push the batter squarely into the prepped pan and heat for 20 minutes. Remove and set on a heat-resistant surface while mixing the filling.

4. Zest 1 lemon in a dish and add the juice from all 3 lemons. Add the remaining 3/4 cup almond flour and mix well.

5. Add 1 egg and cream into the mixture, repeating for all the eggs.

| INGREDIENTS | STEPS FOR COOKING |
|---|---|

6. Finally, add the allulose (3/4 cup) and salt (1/8 teaspoon) and incorporate thoroughly.

7. Transfer the filling to the cooled baking pan and heat on the stove for 25 more minutes.

8. Remove and dust the top with allulose and garnish with a slice of lemon, if preferred.

# COCONUT NO-BAKE COOKIES

Time required:
10 minutes

Servings: 20

## INGREDIENTS

*1 cup melted coconut oil*

*½ cup Monk fruit sweetened maple syrup or your favorite*

*3 cups shredded unsweetened coconut flakes*

## STEPS FOR COOKING

1. Cut out a sheet of parchment paper and place it on a cookie tray.
2. Combine all of the fixings.
3. Run your hands through some water from the tap and shape the mixture into small balls. Arrange them on the pan around one to two inches apart.
4. Press the balls down to form a cookie and refrigerate until firm.
5. It will stay fresh covered for up to 7 days (room temperature). Store in the fridge for up to a month or frozen for up to two months.

# CHOCOLATE CAKE FROM THE CUP

Time required:
10 minutes

Servings: 01

## INGREDIENTS

*1 egg*
*2 tbsp ground hazelnuts*
*1 tbsp coconut oil*
*1 tbsp honey*
*1 pinch of salt*
*1 teaspoon cocoa*

## STEPS FOR COOKING

1. First, preheat the oven to 200 degrees.
2. Then mix all the ingredients together with a fork or in a large mug and cover with aluminum foil and place them in the oven for about 10 minutes.

# Baked Apples in a Chocolate Coating

Time required:
35 minutes

Servings: 30

## INGREDIENTS

*90g almonds*

*6 dates*

*180g cashew nuts*

*2 apples*

*1 lemon*

*1 tbsp honey*

*1 teaspoon cinnamon*

*100g chocolate*

## STEPS FOR COOKING

1. First, soak the almonds and cashew nuts in water overnight.

2. Grate the almonds, dates, and cinnamon in the food processor as small as possible.

3. Line a flat form with parchment paper and press the dough flat on the bottom, then put the mold in the freezer for 20 minutes.

4. Meanwhile, rub the lemon peel off and squeeze the lemon. Puree the apples, cashews, and honey with the juice and zest of the lemon, then spread the mixture on the bottom of the mold.

5. Return the mold to the freezer for 40 minutes; in the meantime, melt the chocolate in a water bath.

6. Now cut dominoes out of the shape and then coat them with the liquid chocolate.
7. Briefly put them in the refrigerator to cool down.

# BROWNIES

Time required:
55 minutes

Servings: 12

## INGREDIENTS

1 (16 ounce) j ar creamy roasted almond butter

2 eggs

1¼ cups raw honey

1 tablespoon pure vanilla extract

½ cup unsweetened cacao powder

½ teaspoon sea salt

1 teaspoon baking soda

1 cup dark chocolate chips (72¾ or higher)

## STEPS FOR COOKING

1. Preheat your oven to 325 degrees F.
2. Start with a large bowl and stir the almond butter until smooth.
3. To the butter, add the eggs, honey, and vanilla and mix well.
4. Now add the cacao powder, salt, and baking soda and blend completely.
5. Gently fold in the chocolate chips.
6. Pour the brownie mixture into a lightly greased 9" x 13" baking dish.
7. Bake at 325 degrees for 35-40 minutes.
8. Allow to cool before slicing.

# BLACKBERRY COBBLER

Time required:
45 minutes

Servings: 06

## INGREDIENTS

*1 pint fresh blackberries or defrosted blackberries*

*¼ cup raw honey*

*½ cup almond flour*

*½ teaspoon arrowroot powder*

*½ teaspoon sea salt*

*½ teaspoon baking soda*

*1 teaspoon baking powder*

*1 teaspoon ground cinnamon*

*1 teaspoon ground nutmeg*

*½ cup almond or coconut milk*

## STEPS FOR COOKING

1. Preheat your oven to 350 degrees F.
2. Lightly grease an 8" x 8" baking dish with olive oil or coconut oil.
3. Place the blackberries in the baking dish and drizzle with the honey.
4. In a separate bowl, mix the almond flour, arrowroot, salt, baking soda, baking powder, cinnamon and nutmeg.
5. Add the almond or coconut milk and vanilla to the dry ingredients and mix well.
6. If batter is too dry, slowly add more milk until a smooth consistency is obtained.
7. Pour the batter over the blackberries and place in the oven.
8. Bake for 25-30 minutes.

| INGREDIENTS | STEPS FOR COOKING |
|---|---|
| *1 teaspoon pure vanilla extract* | 9. Remove from the oven when the crust is browned. |